CW00967920

A secondary teacher's guide

Teaching teenagers with chronic illnesses

Jenny Ollerenshaw

Teaching teenagers with chronic illnesses:
A secondary teacher's guide

Jenny Ollerenshaw

Published by Advance Materials Ltd., 41 East Hatley,
Sandy, Bedfordshire, SG19 3JA, U.K.

www.advancematerials.co.uk

Other books in the series

Teaching children with chronic illnesses:
A primary teacher's guide
978 0 9927056 1 9

First published 2014
© Advance Materials Ltd. 2014

British Library Cataloguing-in-Publication Data

A catalogue record for this book is available from the British Library

Printed in the UK by Cambrian Printers Ltd

ISO-14001 accredited with award-winning Environmental
Management Systems

Printed on FSC mixed sources paper.

- Pulp from an FSC-certified forest
- Controlled Sources, which exclude unacceptable forestry

Chain of custody number TT-COC-2200

www.fsc-uk.org

Cover and book designer: Glen Darby

Editor: Carey Senter Associates

ISBN: 978 0 9927056 0 2

Teaching teenagers with chronic illnesses

Jenny Ollerenshaw

CONTENTS

© Advance Materials Ltd. 2014

"I'm tired of trying to explain to friends, doctors, strangers and teachers about my symptoms, my coping methods and my dietary restrictions. Explaining these things to people is similar to revisiting any other negative experience."

INTRODUCTION

In most of your classes it is quite likely that you will have one or more students with special needs such as ADHD, behavioural problems, mobility or sight problems, etc. These are the high-visibility students. They make their presence felt and it is impossible not to notice them. They demand your time and attention.

It is just as likely that you will also be teaching students who have chronic 'invisible' illnesses. In all likelihood they will not stand out in the same way, and will do everything they can to try to 'hide' the fact that they are ill, so as to fit in with their peers and not draw attention to themselves. These students easily pass unnoticed, as they don't usually demand a lot of attention. Such students can easily slip off the radar of busy teachers in busy classes, who are constantly under pressure.

As a former teacher bringing up a teenager who has been chronically ill since early childhood, I know that I would have been a much more supportive teacher to students with chronic illnesses had I known what I now know. This book aims to give you some understanding of the needs and lives of these students, and a glimpse of how the way you interact with these students can have a huge impact on their daily lives and those of their families.

Looking to establish a gold standard for support

In the writing of this book, dozens of young people came forward not only to give their forthright opinions about their experiences, but also to try and draw a picture of what a gold standard of support for them might look like.

With your help, and that of thousands of other, supportive, caring teachers, we hope that chronically ill students in future will be able to enjoy school, and reach their full emotional and educational potential.

There follow are a couple of testimonies from young people who have gone through their school lives while coping with chronic illness. Be warned, that they don't make comfortable reading. These young people have been left angry and not a little bitter by their overwhelmingly, though not entirely, negative experiences. Like you, they are anxious to try and ensure that the experiences of chronically ill students in the future should be better.

Two testimonies from chronically ill young people

An 18-year-old student, who has Eosinophilic Colitis

Illness isn't a pleasant subject for me. I've had a pick and mix assortment of medical problems since I was born, including severe gastro-oesophageal reflux, eosinophilic colitis, multiple food allergies, fatigue and gall stones. I'm tired of having to explain my assorted conditions to the people I meet. I'm tired of trying to explain to friends, doctors, strangers and teachers about my symptoms, my coping methods and my dietary restrictions. Explaining these things to people is similar to revisiting any other negative experience. It is painful, disheartening, tiring and often embarrassing. However I will try here to give a brief outline of my extensive medical history.

When I was a toddler my parents noticed that I smelled of vomit regularly. When asked about it I said "it's just one of my sickies", under the impression that everybody regurgitated into their mouths regularly. I was taken to a specialist who declared that I had a severe case of gastro-oesophageal reflux and that the lining of my oesophagus was being eroded by the acid. Shortly afterwards, at the age of 5, I underwent a fundoplication – an operation which created an artificial valve at the top of my stomach to prevent acid from coming back up. After the dust had settled on this procedure it was discovered that I had eosinophilic colitis. To this day I don't understand this condition properly, but given that the majority of medical practitioners seem to disagree on what it is I don't feel too bad about my ignorance. What I can tell you is that it's something to do with a surplus of a certain kind of white blood cell and that it makes me feel terrible.

I experience the following known symptoms of this condition:

● headaches ● stomach aches ● fatigue ● dizziness ● nausea

In addition, I also experience:

● bitterness ● anger ● stress ● depression ● lethargy ● bad grades

Since being diagnosed I have been passed from specialist to specialist with little improvement in my condition. I've tried countless medications and treatments but with little success.

Not every teacher has the time to learn the medical details of every student. Not every teacher has the experience to know that sometimes their eyes are not the best way of diagnosing. Not every teacher has the discretion to handle medical matters sensitively especially when the student is surrounded by their peers. Not every teacher has the humility to accept that they might not know best on a subject. I've had too many teachers attribute my not being able to function inside and outside of lessons to discipline problems or laziness. It is damaging for an adolescent's self-esteem if they are assumed to be lying about sensitive matters. The most helpful advice I could give a teacher is to be empathetic and to accept that sometimes your judgement is not necessarily the best. When it feels like my brain is on fire you won't always be able to see it on my face. I don't always appear pale and gaunt when I feel as if I'm going to keel over.

My worst experience in the education system was in my final two years of school. I had been dealing with one teacher in a physical subject that involved music and dance all year. She hadn't been understanding, she made unpleasant comments about me to the class when I wasn't in lessons, she harried me over missed lessons and missed pieces of work, and actually referred me to the discipline department over my absences. Whenever I asked to leave a lesson due to being unwell she would emphasise to me how important the lesson was and would ask me if I couldn't just stay and watch for the rest of the day. I knew better than anyone the consequences of missing a lesson, and would never have *chosen* to be absent. If I attended another teacher's lesson later the same day after going to the medical room to rest in her lesson she would interrogate me. I'm positive that if I had been in a wheelchair, or had a well-known condition she wouldn't have been so awful towards me. But the worst came when one of my friends in the year below me who suffers from epilepsy came to this same teacher to ask if she would be able to take the subject due to it being physically demanding. While discussing this with the teacher my friend mentioned me and mentioned how hard I had found it to cope with the amount of work. The teacher said "Oh but there's nothing wrong with him". I was shocked and hurt – it is obviously inappropriate to even have those sentiments when she'd been told about my medical problems, let alone to voice them to another student.

There were, however, teachers who made my life easier through every stage of my education. Those who praised my efforts despite my disadvantages, those who didn't ask too many questions in front of a class full of my peers and those who helped me to catch up on missed work all helped me immensely. But there were many more teachers who lacked any empathy, didn't treat me with respect and didn't take my illness seriously, teachers who, when I was severely fatigued told me that "*all* of the students and teachers are tired at this time of year" or that I should "really try harder not to miss lessons".

But after spouting so much doom and gloom I'd like to leave you with a happy memory from my education. I had a Physical Education teacher who never made me feel bad about missing a lesson. He seemed to recognise my enthusiasm and frustration at not always being able to join in. He had a variety of suggestions as to how I could be active in the lesson even if I was too sick to actually do the sport – I could be the referee, for example. If I was too unwell to be standing in the cold he would let me read in the library instead. But the thing that left me with the fondest memory was one day when I was about 15 and feeling well enough to be in school but not well enough to take part in the lesson. While the rest of the class was playing tennis he taught me to juggle with tennis balls.

A student now in her early 20's, with M.E.

Chronic illness. Where do I begin?

I was 14 years old when I fell down the stairs, head over heels down the rain-covered concrete at school. I got up, shaken, but said I was fine, though my friends said they were sure I'd hit my head. This fall may somehow have been the cause of what was to come, due to a shock into adrenaline overdrive, though perhaps this is just a grasping-at-straws story explanation thrown at my illness in desperate retrospect. Nevertheless, it was that summer that I started to get the headaches, occasional at first then more and more frequent until I woke up and went to bed in pain, every single day.

These headaches were soon followed by a plethora of other symptoms: sensitivity to light and sound, heat and cold, difficulty in concentrating, loss of appetite, but most of all an endless, heavy, overwhelming tiredness, a fatigue not alleviated, it seemed, by any amount of sleep or rest. In fact, cruelly, I found it difficult to sleep in spite of, even because of, my exhaustion. 'Just go to bed earlier' is advice which is unhelpful, at best.

Over the next 18 months I went to appointment after appointment, doctor after doctor, test after test, until eventually, everything else ruled out, I was diagnosed with M.E. A cop-out, it felt like, a description of my symptoms rather than a promise of treatment or cure. 'She'll grow out of it', one doctor said. 'Just muddle along as best you can', said another. This was exactly what I had been doing and, resigned, this is what I continued to do. The occasional 'miracle-cure' came and went, most notably something called the 'Lightning Technique' which only succeeded in making me feel that if it wasn't working, it must be my fault, I mustn't be doing it right.

M.E. is what one could call an 'invisible' illness – it has no distinct physical manifestations – you don't 'look ill'. Ironically, it was only when, due to the loss of appetite induced by M.E. (I just couldn't find the energy to make myself eat), I lost a scary amount weight that people began to take notice. Only when I was dangerously thin was I offered proper medical help rather than having to chase it or fend for myself. An illness must be visible, it seems, to be treated like an illness. Furthermore, as many symptoms of a low body weight are also common in M.E. sufferers, it was assumed that all my problems would be alleviated with a large slice of cake. Unsurprisingly, when I regained the weight, struggling through mealtimes despite no appetite, the headaches, tiredness, etc. remained. However, as I no longer 'looked' ill, to the wider world I was 'better'.

And for those with a chronic illness, how you appear to the wider world matters. A lot. Strangely enough, I never wanted to be seen as 'ill' but at the same time I wanted my illness to be recognised. At school I never wanted to stand out from my peers, perhaps even putting more effort than most into my schoolwork, overcompensating in an effort to keep up. This of course appeared to teachers like I was doing fine, like there was nothing wrong. To them, I may as well have been making it up! All you want, as a teenager, is to blend in, not to be singled out, but for those with a chronic illness there is also a desire for somebody to acknowledge that it is a struggle for you, that your efforts are noticed but not made a fuss of.

The effort to fit in extends to friendships too. It was not that I wanted to be the *same* as everybody else – I have always been my own person, 'different' in the clothes that I wear, studying Fine Art at university – but I hated not being able to keep up with my peers, found it frustrating to be defeated by their hectic social schedules. So I would turn up to the parties, smile the smiles – I could have been any other young person to the unknowing observer. Yet what they never see is me at home, at my worst, without the brave-faced mask I put on for the world. I felt so inadequate for being exhausted by what was normal activity for others, even resented the extra lifts my parents gave me to enable me to see my friends without the tiring cycle-ride into town. I didn't want to be treated differently, wanted to be independent. I hated always being the 'boring' one who went home early or didn't go out at all. I feel even now like I missed out a large part of my growing up, my (at the risk of sounding melodramatic) formative years, thanks to M.E. My parents gave me the best help they could in the situation we were in, but I am still learning to be independent and look after myself in my early twenties.

The effect my illness has had on my family breaks my heart sometimes. My parents' constant worry and concern, the strain it put on them, the effect it has had on my three siblings, always having to make allowances, perhaps feeling like I got more than my share of attention. But I never *wanted* the extra attention, I didn't *choose* to be ill, to be the 'needy' one – I would give anything to be normal, just like them.

This effort to be 'normal' is also tied, for me, to a fear of giving up. At school, as well as at university, I was advised by doctors to take time out to rest, but I felt that if I let up the effort to keep up, to keep going, if I stopped just for a minute then I would never be able to get back up again. The momentum was keeping me going, the energy I lacked I tried to replace with sheer determination. So, paradoxically, I probably do more than I should just to keep going with daily life, which is something that must seem to others like there is absolutely nothing wrong. Mine is, after all, an 'invisible' illness. If you can't see it, it's not there, right?

" I hate being different from everyone
else. I always try to keep up with
everyone so that probably makes me ill
more. I don't want to be left behind. "

AS A TEACHER, WHAT DO I NEED TO KNOW?

What is a chronic illness and how can I recognise it?

A chronic illness is one which persists for a long time or constantly recurs and is rarely able to be completely cured. It usually requires ongoing management or treatment. It is not necessarily an illness that is critical or dangerous (although some chronic illnesses are life-threatening). A young person with a chronic illness may have periods where they are well or comparatively well, but they always live with the condition. Chronic illness affects the young person not only physically, but emotionally, in terms of their academic performance and their relationships with their peers and with their family.

Approximately 17% of all students under the age of 18 suffer from a chronic illness that affects their performance in school (Cox, Halloran, Homan, Welliver, & Mager, 2008[1]). This means that any one time, you are likely to have at least one child in your class with a chronic illness of one kind or another. There are more students with chronic illnesses than ever before because advances in medical care mean that children who in the past might not have survived through infancy or childhood are now surviving and living with chronic conditions.

In this book we are going to concentrate on 'invisible' chronic illnesses – i.e. those that do not have an obvious outward manifestation (the young person does not use a wheelchair, and does not have obvious physical difficulties or disabilities, etc.). Invisible chronic illnesses include many common and uncommon conditions. In the course of the research for this book we talked to young people with the following illnesses: Diabetes, Epilepsy, M.E. (Chronic Fatigue Syndrome), Crohn's disease, Cystic Fibrosis, Juvenile arthritis, Lupus, Ehlers Danlos Syndrome, Hirschsprung's Disease, Cyclical Vomiting Syndrome, Bronchiectasis, Eosinophilic Gastrointestinal Disease, Kartagener's Syndrome, and Pancreatic disorder.

Unless they have had first- or second-hand experience of chronic illness most people wrongly assume that, if a young person has a chronic illness, there is bound to be some outwardly visible sign of it. If they can't 'see it', they are often tempted to think – at best – that the young person is not ill at the moment or – at worst – that they are just lazy or pretending to be ill to get out of class. This can even occur when all the medical evidence clearly confirms that the young person *is* ill.

The most important thing to understand and remember is that in most cases you simply cannot tell by looking at a young person whether (s)he has a chronic illness or not. A great number of young people suffer from 'invisible' chronic illnesses that are exactly that – invisible. The fact that there is nothing to see does not mean that the young person is not ill. This is perhaps the hardest but most important thing to remember about such young people.

5-year old's response to hearing somebody say that he doesn't look ill: "But unless they have X-ray eyes and can look into your body, how can they know?"

"One of my teachers is always telling me that I look fine. That makes me feel as if she's saying she doesn't believe that I'm sick."

"I feel ill all the time. Even when I'm smiling I feel ill. Most days I just want to snuggle up at home and wish it all away."

> **KEY MESSAGE:** You cannot tell that a young person is chronically ill just by looking at him/her. Don't be tempted to think that you can make a 'visual diagnosis'.

What is the difference between an acute illness and a chronic one?

Acute illness is the term used to describe an illness or medical problem that begins and progresses rapidly, and may well be over very quickly. Most of us are very familiar with acute illnesses of the latter sort, and how young people respond to them. A headache, a stomach upset, a cold or fever – all of these are common acute illnesses in which young people who are normally fit and well suddenly find themselves unwell. As they are unused to feeling unwell, they often react in a very visible way – they express or show pain or discomfort. They may become withdrawn, listless, irritable or upset. In short, they behave in a way that is unusual for them, and it is very obvious to people around them that there is something wrong.

When we think of illness, most of us automatically think of this type of illness and expect to see this very visible reaction in the 'patient'. *Chronic illness differs from this in two respects.*

First, young people who have been ill for a long time learn to live with their symptoms and to get on with their lives as far as possible. In order to get through life they need to find a way of ensuring that their illness doesn't dominate their existence more than is necessary.

Second, the vast majority of young people desperately want to 'fit in' and be seen as 'normal' by their peers and the world at large. Most don't want to stand out and *certainly* don't want to be defined by their illness. Hence they may try to hide symptoms to give the appearance of not being ill.

Both of these factors mean that young people with 'invisible' chronic illnesses are likely to disappear 'under the radar' unless a genuine effort is made to be aware of their challenges.

"I plan when I go to school so my days and resting are based around that and so my teachers and principal see me at my 'best' if you can even call it that. They do not see you all the time. I feel like I have a guard up when I'm out because I don't just want to be seen as that sick person. They really do not see what goes on when you're at your worst. When you're at your worst you normally stay at home and obviously they don't see you when you're at home."

"I hate being different from everyone else. I always try to keep up with everyone so that probably makes me ill more. I don't want to be left behind. Otherwise I genuinely don't care what people think, but in that respect I don't want to be different."

> **KEY MESSAGE: D**on't expect chronically ill young people to react and behave in the same way as acutely ill young people. Despite being ill they may look perfectly 'normal' and 'well'.

'But she/he looks so well!'

The single most common comment that we got from young people who we interviewed about chronic illness was that teachers at school didn't believe that they were ill, often going so far as to comment that they 'didn't *look* ill'. It is perfectly possible that the teacher intends this to be a reassuring comment, offering support to the fragile ego and body image of an adolescent. But it would seem that just as often, it isn't a compliment but a questioning – a disbelief and mistrust on the part of the teacher, who is labouring under the misapprehension that if there were 'really something wrong' there would be something to see in the physical demeanour or behaviour of the young person.

All of your students with chronic illness, will have well-documented diagnoses from medical professionals. These should be accepted.

"For my teachers, if I didn't look ill I wasn't ill. Why don't they believe me?"

> **KEY MESSAGE:** Accept the diagnosis of the medical professionals.

'' Compared to what's happening inside you, education can seem trivial but there's an expectation from school that your learning will take a priority. **''**

THE IMPACT OF A CHRONIC ILLNESS ON A YOUNG PERSON

Having a chronic illness can have a huge impact on a young person at a time when they also have to cope with all the usual challenges of adolescence: growing up physically and emotionally, becoming more independent inside and outside of their families, coping with the stresses of study and exams, preparing for further education and career/work choices, developing supportive peer relationships and a social life, etc. In the hustle and bustle of the school environment this is something that can easily be forgotten or overlooked.

Common physical and psychological effects of chronic illness

Pain

Pain is a symptom that affects many chronically ill young people to a greater or lesser degree. Despite the great advances in medicine many conditions do not respond well to pain-relief medications, meaning that young people may well experience pain on a very regular basis, whether it is constant or intermittent, without recourse to effective pain management. Pain will almost certainly affect mental well-being and can also disrupt sleep patterns. One of the very frustrating things is that the pain can often be unpredictable, with no discernible pattern to it, which can leave the young person feeling very vulnerable as they feel as if they have no control over what happens to their body and are unable to predict how they are going to feel at any point.

As explained already, one often expects it to be evident that someone is in pain, but in all likelihood chronic illness in a young person will not be immediately obvious. When it is particularly bad they may become withdrawn and very quiet, or conversely they may become agitated. They may find it difficult to concentrate and/or become very fatigued. They may also find that they become extra sensitive to light or noise.

In the classroom, it is best to take your lead from the student.

If they prefer to stay in the classroom and do what they can, let them. But, likewise, if they ask to leave the classroom, do trust them to make that decision. Resist the temptation to ask them if they're 'sure', or if they don't want to try for a bit longer. They are probably *very* sure by the time they ask to leave. The chances are that they are really quite fed up about having to ask, and about drawing attention to themselves, and have already held out as long as they can before asking. Questioning the decision will not only draw attention to the student, but will make them feel that you are doubting them.

"When I'm in a lot of pain I find it really difficult to concentrate in class. I prefer to stay in the classroom so that at least I can pick up a bit of what's going on, but I just want to be left alone. I don't want to answer questions or be asked to get involved in practical lessons, but some teachers don't understand and say that if I'm in the classroom then I've got to do everything."

"When I say I need to leave the class because the pain is really bad then some teachers always say 'Are you sure you can't stay for the last hour, because it's really important that you do. Why don't you see how you feel in 10 minutes?' I know when I need to leave. I know how important my lessons are and I don't leave just for the fun of it. At my school we have quite a few kids who fake being ill which doesn't help the people who are actually ill, but they should know by now that I have a genuine illness and not treat me like the fakers."

"Sometimes my games teacher says that I'm skiving games but I'm not. There are just some days when it really hurts even to walk, so I can't do games. But mostly my teachers just sort of ignore the fact that I have a problem and let me get on with my work."

"It's really difficult to plan ahead to go out with my friends or my family because I never know if I'm going to be well enough when the time comes."

> **KEY MESSAGE:** It can be difficult to trust students to manage pain in the way that works best for them, but they know their own physical limitations, and need your support to manage their symptoms in class.

Worry

For young people with chronic illnesses, worry and distress may be quite significant, particularly in those who have had a very recent diagnosis. They are facing a frightening future and often feel very alone amidst their peers who, in contrast, seem to have insubstantial concerns. For some young people their treatment (in or out of hospital) can be prolonged, painful, frightening and place huge restrictions on their lives.

Medication and side-effects

On top of this, the side effects of medication can often interfere with a student's performance at school. These include:

- decreased attention span and ability to concentrate,
- impaired learning,
- drowsiness from poor quantity or quality of sleep, or from the effects of medication,
- lowered energy levels and stamina,
- irritability,
- nausea and
- appearance changes (e.g. weight gain, hair loss or excess hairiness).

Here, communication between home and school is vital so that teachers are aware of changes in medications and changes in symptoms that may have an impact on the young person on a day-to-day basis at school. If you are aware of this, you can then make the necessary allowances, or just be understanding when appropriate.

Fatigue

Fatigue is a symptom that accompanies many chronic illnesses and can be an extremely debilitating and draining problem. Fatigue is not the same thing as normal tiredness, which is relieved by rest and sleep. The fatigued person can feel as if they are wearing a 'heavy suit' which prevents them from moving normally and carrying out daily activities with ease. Tasks such as climbing stairs or even just walking can be hugely draining and leave the person severely exhausted. You may see a chronically fatigued student walk a short distance and just assume that if they can walk they must be fine. But it may be that that distance is the furthest that they can walk that day. If they're able to walk for 10 minutes today it doesn't necessarily mean that they can walk for 20 minutes, or walk for even 5 minutes tomorrow. Levels of fatigue can vary enormously from day to day. Furthermore, it is not just physical activities that are fatiguing. Concentrating, talking, socialising, etc. can all be exhausting to someone who is severely fatigued.

Physical fatigue can also be accompanied by mental fatigue, which means it is difficult to concentrate, with the brain feeling 'foggy' and uncoordinated. Long-term fatigue can lead to other symptoms such as dizziness, headaches, blurred vision, apathy, impaired judgement, indecisiveness, loss of appetite, short-term memory impairment and poor immune system function. If you have never suffered from fatigue, imagine that you've had serious and uninterrupted jet lag for several months, are unable to sleep at night, and are forced to wear a heavy suit day and night.

"The fatigue is always there, like a big black oppressive cloud weighing me down. It just makes it harder to go about my everyday life. Everything takes longer, seems like so much more of a task. I often zone out from exhaustion – I feel as though I am not really there, just watching my life go by at a pace I can't keep up with."

KEY MESSAGE: The only way to combat chronic fatigue is to rest. You can help by reducing the quantity of work in favour of quality of learning, and by being as flexible as possible about schedules and support.

Depressive symptoms, low mood and anxiety

While many young people are well adapted and resilient, having a chronic illness does put a young person at increased risk of psychological problems compared with their healthy peers. Young people with M.E., fibromyalgia, migraine, and epilepsy are at particular risk of developing depressive symptoms. It is not difficult to see why:

- Symptoms such as pain can limit a young person's activities, which can upset them and cause them to feel different from their peers,

- If their peers are aware of their illness they may be treated differently, which can cause embarrassment and anxiety,

- Medications may cause or aggravate low mood,

- The prescribed treatment may be very difficult to follow. Adolescents who have to make major life adjustments to follow their treatment plan may find themselves no longer able to participate in activities with their peers. This can cause great distress and despair. If they have to rely on other people to remind them to take medication or to help with treatment this can also make them feel dependent and lower their self-esteem,

- The symptoms of many chronic illnesses fluctuate, being more or less pronounced at different times, depending on a whole host of factors that are beyond the control of the patient. This can lead to a feeling of helplessness and of not having any control over their life, which can in turn lead to depressive symptoms,

- Missing a lot of school can lead to the disruption of friendship groups, leading to a lack of friends and a sense of isolation,

- Chronically ill young people may in some cases find themselves subject to abuse – verbally or on social media,

- Having a chronically ill child places great pressure on the whole family and can frequently put stresses on a marriage, when each partner copes in a different way. Young people are very sensitive to stresses and conflict within their family and may feel that these difficulties are their 'fault',

- Anxiety disorders are also higher in children and young people with chronic medical illness, with rates ranging from 7% to 40% (Maryland Pao & Abigail Bosk, 2011[2]). Anxiety symptoms include feeling worried, tense or fearful, bouts of crying and feeling unable to switch off thoughts, and can be accompanied by physical symptoms such as nausea, shakiness, loss of appetite, raised heart rate and insomnia. Anxiety symptoms can develop as a direct result of the specific illness or medications (e.g. shortness of breath in heart disorders) but also as a response to being ill or in hospital and having to undergo frequent painful medical procedures.

It is important to appreciate that in the majority of cases depressive symptoms develop as secondary symptoms to the primary chronic illness. Curing the depressive symptoms, while very welcome, will not make the young person physically well.

"Depression is a difficult thing to talk about to both friends and teachers because of the fear of not being taken seriously."

"Compared to what's happening inside you, education can seem trivial but there's an expectation from school that your learning will take a priority."

"My friends often say 'Oh I'm really depressed' but they don't have a clue what depression really means."

Some chronic illnesses are life-limiting and can have a significant impact on a young person's motivation to struggle on at school. Gentle encouragement and understanding is key to helping students navigate through these feelings on what can be a daily basis.

"Why should I bother studying? I'm not going to live long enough to get a job anyway."

It can be difficult to sort out depressive and anxiety symptoms from 'ordinary' everyday worries about family, school and friendships which young people face. However it is very important to be alert and to take all symptoms seriously so that professional help can be sought as appropriate.

> **KEY MESSAGE:** Take students with depressive and anxiety symptoms seriously. They can have serious consequences. Young people with chronic illnesses have plenty of factors contributing towards feeling low and anxious, so need support and understanding.

Social and developmental effects of chronic illness

Risk taking

Risk taking and experimentation is a normal developmental feature of adolescence but this can be more much more difficult for young people with a chronic illness; the medical condition may increase dependence on parents and doctors for medication, hospital visits and treatment. In turn, worried parents can find it hard to 'let go' of their sick child and allow them the independence they'd like.

Relationships with peers

Relationships with peers can also be tricky for young people with health problems. They are likely to become much more sensitive about how their illness is perceived by their friends. Frequent absence from school can mean that they are not integrated into specific friendship groups, lose touch with close friends or simply do not have any close friends at all. They may also find it difficult to identify with their peers when their own daily concerns are so different from those of their friends. As they see their friends moving forward, chronically ill young people can feel left behind, even abandoned, and can sometime experience feelings of failure in keeping up with their peers.

"All of my school friends know that I get sick and they understand that I go to the hospital but I don't think they really know what it feels like to be sick. Some of them have been in hospital for, like, one night and one of them has asthma but they don't know what it's like to have medicines and stuff every day and spend loads of time in hospital."

"I think it does put pressure on friendships. It's tough on the other person if you're the one who always needs looking after. I hate admitting that I need help."

"People in my class make such a fuss when they have a sore throat or a headache, and they take the day off just because there's something pathetic wrong with them!"

Self-esteem

At a time when personal appearance and body image is crucial and 'fitting in' is of paramount importance, adolescents with health problems may find ordinary teenage concerns are multiplied and amplified. Illnesses and treatments that affect their appearance can cause crippling self-esteem issues. Even small differences in appearance that may not be very obvious to others, can seem disproportionally significant to teenagers at an age when young people in general, ill or not, are extremely aware of and often dissatisfied with their appearance. If as a teacher you are sensitive to these extra pressures that chronically ill young people may be facing you will be in a position to give them extra understanding or support which could make a big difference to them. It is important, too, to be aware of any teasing or bullying around the young person's physical appearance.

"When I was on steroids I got really fat and my face puffed up and was covered in spots. I felt really ugly and didn't want to go out of the house. I didn't want anyone to look at me. I just wished I could die."

KEY MESSAGE: The 'ordinary' strains of adolescent life can be an even bigger struggle for young people with chronic illnesses, but you won't necessarily see any of it on the surface. They just want to be like everybody else, so will do their best to fit in or hide their illness.

" I don't know how I would have managed at school, particularly with my exams, if it hadn't been for someone in the school office who took an interest and really listened to me. "

WHAT CAN WE DO AS A SCHOOL?

There is no doubt that meeting the educational, social and emotional needs of chronically ill young people is time consuming, but when done well, it can significantly improve the quality of life and the academic performance of the young person.

A number of schools have an excellent record of looking after young people with chronic illnesses, and the key elements these schools share include: key staff, excellent communication, good information, flexibility, and a will to make it work.

They also tend to share a number of structural elements that have been put in place, and which are explicitly supported by management and staff.

Key support staff

In the schools that support chronically ill students best, there is single key member of staff assigned to each student, so that the student has someone with whom they can build a long-term and trusting relationship. In many cases this will be a member of the Special Needs' Department, but some schools also use other members of staff very effectively in this role. The important thing is that the key member of staff should be able to provide continuity of care over several years, rather than having a different member of staff each year.

This key person is very valuable to the student, not least because endlessly having to talk to lots of different people about their illness is both exhausting and embarrassing.

Main responsibilities of the key staff member

The key support staff member has a number of responsibilities:

- meeting with the student, ideally *before* they start at the school, and then very regularly throughout the student's career at the school, to assess progress and to talk to them about how they are coping,

- creating summary information sheets or records, and updating and fine-tuning the information on a regular basis,

- deciding with parents and the student when new information needs to be disseminated to staff,

- ensuring that information is disseminated appropriately, and that sensitive information is made available securely to selected staff,

- sometimes, co-ordinating work being sent home and issues such as extensions to deadlines for homework.

An important aspect of the key staff member being responsible for feeding back to other staff is taking the burden of doing so away from the student, who may otherwise have to explain a development in their condition over and over again to numerous teachers.

Whether this key support staff member also communicates with parents on a regular basis is something that should be decided with the student. Some students prefer to be able to talk to their key member in complete confidence and would rather that another member of staff liaised with their parents when necessary. It should be assumed that personal information that the young person discloses is confidential and should only be shared with their consent. If in doubt, check with the student.

Good access to support staff

The best schools make sure that there is a member of support staff available before, during and immediately after school hours and that young people know where they can go to find that person to get help if necessary. This could be a member of the Special Needs staff, a member of the administrative staff or if the school is lucky enough to have a full time one, the nurse. A crisis can occur at any stage of the day, and if the student knows where to go and who to seek out, everything will run much more smoothly.

"At our school there is a member of the Special Needs Department 'on call' around the clock. We provide a consistent presence and approach, and students can come to us when they need to, knowing that they can just rest if need be, without being interrogated."

Head of Special Needs, school in Cambridge

"I don't know how I would have managed at school, particularly with my exams, if it hadn't been for someone in the school office who took an interest and really listened to me. I think if it hadn't been for her I wouldn't have made it through my last year at school."

Information about chronically ill students

In order to make the necessary adjustments and offer appropriate flexibility to students with medical needs, teachers need to have relevant and appropriate information about them.

Again, in schools where chronically ill students are supported best, this information is set up by staff with explicit responsibility to do so, and it is maintained and used systematically.

The school needs to ask parents and students to give them full information about the young person's condition *before* they start at the school, and to encourage them to keep the school up to date with any changes. The summary information sheets or records which are held centrally need to include:

- the name and description of the condition(s) in both formal and lay terms,
- any *relevant* recent clinical letters,
- a list of common symptoms that the young person may experience and the effects it may have on their behaviour or performance,
- any particular fears or worries that the young person has in relation to their condition or how it affects them,
- a clear indication of what might constitute an emergency, and
- clear instructions of action that needs to be taken.

Disseminating information

The full information should be kept on file centrally in case it should be needed. However it needs to be summarised intelligently and disseminated in an accessible and easily-digestible format to all teachers in the school who have contact with the student. (See appendix on page 44 for an example).

For practical reasons, this is likely to be done by email. In smaller schools the information may be given out orally in a staff meeting where a photo of the student identifies them to all staff, including non-teaching staff and those who do not teach them. Alternatively briefing meetings can be held with teachers about individual students.

Teachers may well need to remind themselves of information about students in the various classes that they teach. It is therefore useful to be able to print off:

- information about a particular student, perhaps in some detail,
- summarised information about the class as a whole, with a key sentence or two for each student with medical needs.

It is equally important that substitute teachers are given relevant medical information for children in each class that they teach, and they may find the pared-down information sheet on each class particularly useful.

Confidentiality is of paramount importance, and sensitive or confidential information should be imparted to specific teachers on a need-to-know basis.

As a teacher, if you don't feel you have enough information or that it is not clear enough, then do ask the person or office in your school that is responsible for collating the information. If it is not clear to you, it won't be clear to others either and it will be the student who loses out.

"The stand-in teachers never know that I'm allowed to go out of the class when I show my card*. I get really embarrassed about all the questions they ask, so unless I'm having a really bad attack I just don't go outside and have a breather when I need it. I'd rather suppress my illness and hide it than have them make such a fuss in front of my friends."

* See page 31 for the 'Out of class pass system'.

> **KEY MESSAGE:** Maintaining up-to-date, relevant information and ensuring that it is made available to all teaching and non-teaching staff is vital. Confidentiality must be respected.

Communication

Parents

Parents of children with chronic illnesses are usually a mine of information. Talk to them. They are the people who know their children best, who live with them on a daily basis, and know how their condition affects them. In the case of rare illnesses, the parents are often far better informed than general practitioners, and may also have a much greater understanding of the illness and its impacts.

Wherever possible, we suggest that you meet with the parents of a chronically ill student, preferably before they come to the school, to gather information and to listen to their concerns and suggestions. Parents all too often feel that they have to 'fight' to get their voice heard by schools and to get the support that their children need. Establishing an atmosphere of cooperation and respect from the outset can go a very long way towards ensuring that the best outcome is achieved for the student and that lines of communication are kept open. It is much easier to resolve problems or disagreements if parents know that from the outset you have genuinely listened to them and shown them that you want to work *with* them.

The young person

Depending on the age of the young person, and the length of their illness, they may have a greater or lesser understanding of the medical details of their condition. For some young people who have been ill all their lives, you may be surprised by their lack of understanding of the specifics of their illness. This can arise when parents give children a simple explanation when they are young, and forget to update them with more details as they get older! For young people who fall ill when they are older, they often have a very good understanding of their illness. However there are no hard and fast rules and it is always useful to ask the young person to explain in their own words, to their key staff member, what they understand about their illness. Remember that in rare cases, parents may have made the decision to keep some details of medical information from the young person. As a teacher one cannot pass judgement on the rights or wrongs of such a decision, but bear in mind that if parents have chosen to do so, the school cannot opt to disclose something that the parents have specifically chosen not tell the young person.

Whether or not the young person has a good medical knowledge of the illness, they will definitely be the person best placed to understand the impact that it has on them. Again, it is recommended that their key staff member talks to them when they first join the school (and subsequently at appropriate intervals) to get their perspective on how the illness affects them, what aggravates it, what eases it, and what they perceive to be their support needs. It is equally important to find out how much they want their classmates to know and if there is anything that they are especially embarrassed or concerned about. Addressing concerns early on will enable the student to relax and consequently to learn better.

"The teachers only get the hospital letters with the long words, but they don't understand what it means to me."

© Advance Materials Ltd. 2014

Medical professionals

Parents are usually sent copies of letters from hospital consultants; these letters vary in how much medical terminology is used. It may sometimes be helpful for schools to see copies of letters from the hospital consultant and while they can be useful, it is not usually necessary that these are kept on record as a matter of course. Unless things are changing at a dramatic rate, the school will not need to see every hospital letter in order to keep up to date with the young person's medical progress. Where a medical letter is needed for the purposes of special arrangements for examinations, for example, it is usually quicker and more efficient simply to ask the parents to request that the young person's general practitioner provides the information.

The Internet

It is very tempting to go to the Internet to look up a diagnosis provided for a particular student. While this can sometimes be enlightening, great caution should be exercised as the general information given on a website about a particular condition may not apply at all to any one particular patient. Every patient is an individual and illnesses can affect patients in very different ways and to varying degrees. You cannot assume that what you read about a particular illness on the Internet applies to the young person who has been diagnosed with that illness

> **KEY MESSAGE:** Gather information from the people who know the student best: primarily the parents and the young person him/herself. Beware of assuming that what you read online applies to the young person that you teach.

'Out-of-class' pass system

A widely used system that helps chronically ill students enormously is where all students with medical needs are provided with an out-of-class pass that enables them to leave the room without questions being asked. They can just show the pass and go.

This system is a very practical way of reducing embarrassment and disruption in the classroom if students need to leave quickly. Many students worry about having to ask if they may leave the class, and also about the questions and public discussion that might follow. This system allows students to go to the quiet room or to the toilet as necessary.

Remember that:

● substitute teachers need to be made aware of the system, and

● all teachers should respect the system, and never make students feel awkward about using it. The whole point is to avoid the 'Do you really need to go?' question. The student really does.

If you suspect that some students are misusing their passes, then the system for allocating them should be reviewed, rather than interrogating each student who uses one. The whole point of the system is to avoid that conversation.

"My bowel doesn't work very well and this makes it difficult for me to get to the toilet on time. I am allowed to go to the toilet as often as I need to without asking and Miss doesn't tell me off like some of the others who go all the time."

Physical spaces

Access to a quiet place

In a busy, noisy school, chronically ill young people will sometimes need a safe, easy-to-access place where they can just rest, take medication or be quiet. Unfortunately many schools do not have such a place for such students.

Ideally, it is a place where the student can just 'be', not a medical room, but rather a room where there is at least one adult present, in case they should wish to talk or need practical help. The room should be easy to get to, preferably without climbing stairs, with the facility to sit or lie down if necessary. If the young person is in pain they might be extra sensitive to light or noise, so dimming the lights and/or giving them access to a pair of noise-cancelling headphones can be very helpful in reducing distress.

Both students and staff should know where the student needs to go if the need arises.

"To go to the medical room in our college you first need to climb two flights of stairs to fetch the key, and then you need to climb the stairs again to return it when you leave. When I'm feeling really bad there's no way I have the energy to do that, so I just don't use the medical room."

"At my secondary school there was a special room I could go to when I couldn't stay in class because the pain was too much for me. I could just rest there, and then when I was ready I went back to the lesson."

"I don't have anywhere to go and sit when I need to, or anywhere private to take my medication."

Bathroom facilities

For students who have bowel or bladder problems, using shared facilities with their peers can be a daily nightmare and a source of enormous anxiety. Giving such students permission to use a designated staff bathroom, away from the student toilets, can go a huge way towards reassuring them and giving them confidence. If there is a bathroom with a shower, so much the better, as accidents can sometimes be very messy and the quickest way to clean up is with a shower.

"If my colostomy pouch leaks I'm allowed to go to a staff toilet where there's a shower, so that I can clean myself up without worrying about everyone else knowing what's happened."

Medical locker

Students with medical needs really benefit from having a personal locker somewhere that is easy to access. Here they can store spare clothes, equipment such as noise-cancelling headphones, eye blind, TENS machine, etc. They can also leave books and kit there if they find it very tiring to carry all their gear around with them during the day.

"Sometimes I use my medical locker for my ordinary stuff, because it's in a much quieter place. The normal lockers are really busy and everyone pushes and shoves. If I'm having a bad day it's easier not to have to fight my way through in the normal locker area."

Training for staff on the difference between acute and chronic illness

All staff need to be trained in the differences between acute and chronic illnesses (see page 14) and to be very aware that their role is not to try to diagnose or judge but to support the student and to facilitate their education despite their illness.

WHAT CAN I DO IN THE CLASSROOM?

As we said earlier, the key to a school providing good support to chronically ill youngsters is excellent communication, flexibility, understanding, and a will to make it work. The same is, of course, true in the classroom, but there are some additional means of supporting these students, which are of enormous help when implemented by classroom teachers, and which, together, can make a huge difference to emotional, physical and education outcomes.

Participation

Students who have regular absences or who often feel under par during lessons may find it difficult to participate fully during lessons and extracurricular activities. It is important to let them do what they can and to accept their limitations. For instance, a student who is really keen on sport but does not have the stamina to play for a full match could play for just the first half. A student who is feeling very unwell in a lesson might just want to listen instead of participating actively. If you trust them to decide what they can and cannot do they will feel much more confident and relaxed, and will get much more out of their learning.

"I wish teachers would understand that sometimes I can only be a fly on the wall in class. I want to listen but I can't be active."

"Recently I joined my school choir and I couldn't go for three weeks because I had been off school with a virus and couldn't sing as I had a chesty cough, and the teacher told me that I should quit choir because I was 'clearly not ready to take responsibility' for my commitments, which made me rather upset. It isn't my fault that having Lupus means I get sick easily."

> **KEY MESSAGE:** Let the student be the judge of the extent to which they can or cannot participate in lessons on a particular day.

Encouragement

Encouragement can go a really long way towards helping young people to feel supported and understood. Knowing that teachers are aware of the challenges that they face and that they are supportive is of huge significance to students. A smile of encouragement, a nod of understanding, a discreet word of praise; all give chronically ill students a real boost and help them to continue in the knowledge that they are not alone. Most of the time big gestures are not necessary – the small, regular notes of encouragement are far more valuable.

"It would have been so nice if for once instead of telling me off for being absent my teacher could have just said how nice it was to see me in school, or if she could have said well done for me coming in when I was feeling so bad."

KEY MESSAGE: A word of encouragement goes a long way.

Agreeing objectives

At a time when schools and teachers are under enormous pressure to improve student performance in examinations, it must not be forgotten that some students may have different objectives to their peers. Some chronically ill students defy all the odds and perform at an outstanding level in examinations. In some cases, this might be at a very great cost to their health. Others, despite having the potential to do extremely well academically, may decide that they are going to set their sights a bit lower in order to maintain a better balance with their health. Depending on the age of the student, this is a decision that might be made with or without their parents, but always in discussion with their key member of staff. It is vital that this discussion takes place. If the school is aware of the goals that individual students have set themselves, appropriate encouragement and support can be offered. These goals should be revisited from time to time to take account of any changes.

"I remember a young lady with cystic fibrosis who became very poorly with added complications in her final year. There was so much focus on whether she was going to get the expected number of GCSEs that we lost sight of (or perhaps weren't able to be satisfied with) the fact that she was happy to have achieved anything at all, at any grade, because the battle to come into school was enough in itself."

Head of Special Needs

Discretion

Teachers who act with discretion can really make a positive difference to the experience of chronically ill students. Check with the student, as they may not want their fellow students to know that they are ill. If they need to go out of class it can be very embarrassing for them if you stop the class to question them in front of their peers.

Similarly, although chronically ill students recognise that teachers need to know about their illness they may well not want to talk about it to you in person. This is often the case where they find the illness embarrassing, but it is equally likely that the student simply does not want to have to relate the ins and outs of their condition, or talk about such a personal matter to yet another person. They may prefer to communicate through their key member of staff.

KEY MESSAGE: Respect the student's right to privacy about their condition. Don't assume that they will be happy to talk about it to you or to others.

Catching up on work

For students who have a lot of absences it is very important to have a system in place that allows them to catch up on work easily. Depending on the nature and length of the absence, there are several ways in which this can be done. If work needs to be sent home, lessons can be emailed and textbooks can be made available for home use if the student does not own them.

Prioritising work

If the student is feeling very ill and does not have much energy then, when it comes to catching up (or dealing with homework), they need to be very clear about what material they absolutely need to know, and what is more peripheral. As a teacher you are best placed to make that decision.

Missing school is stressful enough without having the extra worry of catching up with huge amounts of work. It will be much easier for them to concentrate on what is most important if:

- you have identified the essential parts of the curriculum they should focus on,

- you have noted down when new concepts or topics have been introduced in their absence,

- you have organised a 'study buddy', whose notes they can photocopy (if they can choose their own study buddy, so much the better).

Catching up might be through a lunchtime 'surgery' with you, or with an older and reliable student, or simply through very thorough notes that could also be made available to other students who are struggling. This latter approach may also help the chronically ill student to feel that they are not alone, or any less able than their peers.

Alternatively you might just make your lessons available online or by email.

> **KEY MESSAGE:** Prioritise the work that is really essential to make it easier for them to catch up after absences.

ADVICE FROM THE STUDENTS FOR YOU

What we'd *really* like to say to teachers

Here is some of the advice that young people told us they'd like to give to teachers, about how to treat young people with chronic illnesses.

"What really helps is just for teachers to listen. Some people hear but don't listen, but it's really helpful when they listen and don't put words in your mouth."

17 year old with M.E. (Chronic Fatigue Syndrome)

"Imagine trying to do your job on nearly no sleep and loads of pain."

14 year old with Juvenile Arthritis

"I would tell teachers to get to know a bit about my condition and watch out for the symptoms so that I can get treatment really quickly and then I'll get better quicker. I would tell them to listen to me and call my mum when I say I don't feel well because I don't ever say I'm not well when I'm not, just to get out of school – that would be stupid!"

11 year old with Kartagener's Syndrome

"The advice I'd give teachers is just to acknowledge that we're not making it up!"

17 year old with Bronchiectasis

"Don't make them feel like they have a problem, and encourage them a lot and be supportive. Maybe give them less homework or longer deadlines."

17 year old with Lupus

"People who have chronic illnesses have more stress and are more grouchy, so when people take the mick or don't believe you, it's worse."

15 year old with Ehlers Danlos Syndrome

"Be understanding – how would you feel if it was your son or daughter?"

13 year old with Hirschsprung's Disease

"Don't be too patronising. Treat them normally but with a background of knowledge."

17 year old with a pancreatic disorder

"Don't define us by our illness."

15 year old with Cystic Fibrosis

"Acknowledge that actually I'm making a huge effort to be in school, instead of telling me off for being absent so much."

17 year old with M.E.

"Don't immediately assume that I'm exaggerating when I say how I feel."

17 year old with Eosinophilic Gastrointetinal Disease

"Treat us with respect – we may be ill but we still have feelings."

15 year old with Crohn's disease

"Understand that a chronic illness is unpredictable. Some days or hours I don't feel bad at all and then suddenly out of the blue I can feel really awful. I can't control it which is really frustrating and upsetting."

13-year old with Cyclical Vomiting Syndrome

"Don't forget that just because we're ill doesn't mean that we're different inside. We have lots of extra problems, but we still have the same feelings as everyone else."

15 year old with Diabetes

"Remember that it's important to be friendly and polite to the student you're trying to help."

16 year old with Epilepsy

10 things *not* to say to a chronically ill student

*"But you look so well./You don't **look** ill."* (This makes the student feel as if you don't believe them or as if you're dismissing their illness.)

"You really must try to have fewer absences." (Many chronically ill students make a real effort to come to school even when they are feeling very unwell. They are very aware of the problems that absences cause but are rarely in control of them.)

"Are you sure you need to leave the lesson? Don't you think you could stay for a bit longer?" (Trust the student to know when they need to leave the lesson, and don't interrogate them – especially not in front of the rest of the class.)

"Yes, my cousin/friend had the same thing as you, and she's doing really well now." (The experience of two people with the same or similar diagnosis may be completely different. Telling a student that someone else is doing much better than they are is disheartening and can lead to feelings of failure.)

"Yes, I'm really tired too/Yes, I get headaches too." (Don't presume that you know how the chronically ill student feels or can relate to it. In most cases you won't have experienced anything similar, or for the protracted length of time that they have had to cope with it. By implying that you have similar symptoms you may make them feel as if you are minimising their experience.)

"I wish I could stay at home in bed and rest." (Young people who are off school at home feeling unwell usually want nothing more than to feel well and be able to continue their lives as normal. Such a comment makes them feel as if they're perceived to be at home lazing around when they're off school.)

"I don't know why you're saying you can't do X – you did it yesterday/ last week!" (Chronic illnesses are unpredictable and sufferers often feel very different from one day to another. They may well be able to do something one day but not the next. Pushing them to do something that they say they can't do may lead to serious consequences.)

"Have you tried X remedy/medicine?/ Why don't you just…" (People with chronic illnesses have usually tried every possible avenue for a cure, and seen many health professionals. It can be very wearing to listen to people who know nothing about the condition giving 'quick fix' advice and can be stressful when they expect you to follow up on it.)

"I hope you get well soon!" (This just emphasises to the student that you've really not understood that their condition is chronic and is not going to disappear overnight.)

"Think positive!" (This can sound to the student as if you are dismissing what is a real medical problem or suggesting that it is their own fault that they are ill. It does not recognise the fact that while a lot of the time they may try to be very positive, they have days when they feel really down and upset, which is perfectly normal under the circumstances.)

10 *supportive* things to say to a chronically ill student

"It's lovely to see you in school today!"

"Well done for coming to my lesson/ handing in your homework/completing your coursework – I know things have been hard for you lately."

"I trust your judgement."

"While you were away I set two lots of homework for the class – X and Y. I know that you're going to find it difficult to catch up on all the missed work, so don't worry too much about completing X. Y is much more important, so it would be good if you could spend some time on it. If you don't have time to write a full essay, just think about it and hand me in your thoughts in bullet point form."

"I know that things are tough for you at the moment. I'm sure you'd rather not go through all the details with me, but I'm here if ever you'd like to talk or if you need help with anything that you don't understand in class."

"I hear that you're going to be off for a couple of weeks while you're in hospital. What would you like me to say to the class about it, or would you prefer me not to say anything?"

"That was a really impressive piece of work. I know that things are difficult at the moment for you, so I appreciate how much work you must have put into it!"

(At the end of the lesson when the other students have left the classroom) *"If you've got a lot on with your other subjects at the moment, then don't worry too much about the piece of homework that I've just set, as it's not vital and you obviously understand the principles."*

"Please do tell me or someone else if there are things we can do at school to make things easier for you."

(When there is some flexibility over when an oral exam or practical piece of work has to be done) *"Are you well enough to do the assessment today, or would you prefer to wait until the next date?"*

KEY MESSAGES OVERVIEW

- You cannot tell that a young person is chronically ill just by looking at him/her. Don't be tempted to think that you can make a 'visual diagnosis'.

- Don't expect chronically ill young people to react and behave in the same way as acutely ill young people. Despite being ill they may look perfectly 'normal' and 'well'.

- Accept the diagnosis of the medical professionals.

- It can be difficult to trust students to manage pain in the way that works best for them, but they know their own physical limitations, and need your support to manage their symptoms in class.

- The only way to combat chronic fatigue is to rest. You can help by reducing the quantity of work in favour of quality of learning, and by being as flexible as possible about schedules and support.

- Take students with depressive and anxiety symptoms seriously. They can have serious consequences. Young people with chronic illnesses have plenty of factors contributing towards feeling low and anxious, so need support and understanding.

- The 'ordinary' strains of adolescent life can be an even bigger struggle for young people with chronic illnesses, but you won't necessarily see any of it on the surface. They just want to be like everybody else, so will do their best to fit in or hide their illness.

- Maintaining up-to-date, relevant information and ensuring that it is made available to all teaching and non-teaching staff is vital. Confidentiality must be respected.

- Gather information from the people who know the student best: primarily the parents and the young person him/herself. Beware of assuming that what you read online applies to the young person that you teach.

- Let the student be the judge of the extent to which they can or cannot participate in lessons on a particular day.

- A word of encouragement goes a long way.

- Respect the student's right to privacy about their condition. Don't assume that they will be happy to talk about it to you or to others.

- Prioritise the work that is really essential to make it easier for them to catch up after absences.

APPENDIX

Example of summary of medical needs

Name	Class	Support needed in class	Extra info	Symptoms	Medical needs
		Wears hearing aids and should use radio aid. Seat appropriately for lip reading. Use subtitles with media resources. Check understanding of instructions. Sensitive grouping.	Wear radio mic.	Hearing loss.	Severe hearing impairment.
		May need to eat snack in class to raise blood glucose. Go to support room if feeling very unwell.	Needs to eat little and often during the day and shouldn't consume much sugar. No sugary drinks. Out of class pass.	Can get symptoms of low blood sugar (a bit like a diabetic). Feels weak, shaky and confused.	Dumping syndrome (rapid stomach emptying) following surgery.
		Send to support room if in a lot of pain. Can be very anxious and may need reassurance.	Allowed to use staff toilet and shower next to staff room. Out of class pass.	Tummy aches. Rectal bleeding.	Crohn's disease. (inflammatory bowel disease).
		May need to test blood glucose, and eat snacks in class, or take insulin.	May need to count carbohydrates. Out of class pass.	With low blood glucose (hypo) may get fast heart rate, shakiness, chills, nausea. May also become confused or disorientated, or may appear aggressive.	Diabetic. May need supervision of insulin administration.